MW00423668

This book belongs to:

____